What peop!

The Galli

I absolutely love this book! _ ...as ueen beautifully crafted. It educated and entertained me throughout. The Gallic Cooking Pot is such a witty and wonderfully woven gem of a book and I would highly recommend it.
Liggy Webb, Award-Winning Author and Presenter

The author is turning for us foreigners the key in the lock of the mystery on how to understand French people or "Frenchness". Only a French could do this. The book is humorous and serious all together. Jan Abellan's illustrations achieve the perfect balance: "just right and not too much".
Dr. Dr. h.c. Walter B. Gyger, Retired Swiss Ambassador

This is a succinct and pleasurable read with considerable depth. It imparts a great deal of wisdom for non-French and French people alike, and confirms my conviction that even after decades of living with the French, there's always something new to learn—and of course, to discuss for hours while enjoying a delicious meal together!
Ruth Mastron, MA, Intercultural Specialist, Writer

This easy-to-read book explains how some qualities and specificities can cause misunderstandings. I was particularly interested because I have a PhD in Risk Management...and I happen to be French myself ! I intend to use those skills in my daily life and work.
Julien Chorier, Ultrarunner - Speaker

"Achieving a successful recipe means being light-handed and balanced with the ingredients." As the author shows us, the rule has application well beyond the kitchen. Between gastronomical courses we learn about the Académie Française, Jean Paul Sartre and Simone de Beauvoir. That is the France I, a Cuban-American, have learned to love and admire. A fun book to take with you on vacation!

Dr. Alfred de Zayas, Editor-in-Chief and Founder of the United Nations Society of Writers, Past Président, PEN International Centre Suisse Romand 2006-2009, 2013-2017

The author presents her compatriots with a touch of self-deprecating irony. As a specialist in self-development and conflict resolution, she is experienced in analysing human behaviour. In this book she applies her skills to enable Anglophones get a better understanding of the French mentality — which may seem a little bizarre at times ...

Huguette Junod, Swiss Publisher

As a former rugby player, as well as with my business partners, I know that it's important to go beyond stereotypes to put messages across and have an impact. The Gallic Cooking-Pot does exactly that; it's a very instructive book about French culture and specificities, and a good read : illuminating, for any visitor to France.

Serge Betsen, Former Rugby Player, Coach and Speaker, Founder of Serge Betsen Academy

Marie-José Astre's years of working in the United Nations gives her an in-depth awareness of what is profoundly French. She explains what is specifically French in an easy to read and pleasant format.

Katrina Burrus, PhD, MCC, Leadership catalyst-speaker-author

The Gallic Cooking-Pot

Why can't the rest of the world get on with the French?

The Gallic Cooking-Pot

Why can't the rest of the world get on with the French?

Marie-José Astre-Démoulin

Illustrated by Jan Abellan
Adapted/translated by Caroline Thonger

BUSINESS
BOOKS

Winchester, UK
Washington, USA

JOHN HUNT PUBLISHING

First published by Business Books, 2021
Business Books is an imprint of John Hunt Publishing Ltd., No. 3 East St., Alresford,
Hampshire SO24 9EE, UK
office@jhpbooks.com
www.johnhuntpublishing.com
www.johnhuntpublishing.com/business-books

For distributor details and how to order please visit the 'Ordering' section on our website.

Text copyright: Marie-José Astre-Démoulin 2020

ISBN: 978 1 78904 613 7
978 1 78904 614 4 (ebook)
Library of Congress Control Number: 2020943572

A CIP catalogue record for this book is available from the British Library.

Design: Stuart Davies

UK: Printed and bound by CPI Group (UK) Ltd, Croydon, CR0 4YY
Printed in North America by CPI GPS partners

We operate a distinctive and ethical publishing philosophy in
all areas of our business, from our global network of authors to
production and worldwide distribution.

Contents

Previous Publications

Books

Genève Emois, Editions des sables, 2019
ISBN 978-2-940530-68-7
Le nid vide, récit d'un mal de mère, Favre éditions, 2014
ISBN 978-8289-1430-1
La marmite gauloise, La Boîte à Pandore (to be published in 2020)
ISBN 978-2-87557-387-2

* * *

Essays, poems, in various publications

L'impatience, Les cahiers du sens, Le nouvel Athanor, 2019
ISBN 978-2-35623-088-1
La voie/les voix, Les cahiers du sens, Le nouvel Athanor, 2018
ISBN 9 782356 2308 12
Ex Tempore, United Nations Society of Writers, 2016, 2017,
2018, 2019

* * *

Literary translations from English into French

Efuru, Flora Nwapa, L'Harmattan Publisher,
ISBN 2-85802-959-8
L'accueil du jeune enfant, Collection la vie de l'enfant, ESF
Publisher, ISBN 782710 109426
Par un matin d'automne, Robert Goddard, Belfond Publisher
ISBN 782714 425652, Sonatine ISBN 978-2-355840-48, Le livre de
poche ISBN 2253158364

Un horizon de cristal, Raye Morgan, Editions J'ai Lu,
ISBN 782277 851110
Prisonnière d'un rêve, Sara Chance, Editions J'ai Lu,
IBN 782277 850700
Rêves de paradis, Stephanie James, Editions J'ai Lu,
ISBN782280 851671
Comme une pluie d'étoiles, Cassandra Bishop, Editions J'ai Lu,
ISBN 782277 851011
Au soleil de la passion, Angel Milan, , Editions J'ai Lu,
ISBN 782280 851756
D'abord, vous pleurez, Betty Rollin, Belfond Publisher,
ISBN 978-2-7144-2173-9
Le rêve californien, David Nevin, Belfond Publisher,
ISBN 2.7144.2281.0

* * *

Articles
Numerous articles written in *UN Special* magazine:

Epigraph

How can anyone govern a nation that has two hundred and forty-eight different kinds of cheese, **Charles de Gaulle**

Acknowledgments

A warm thank you to Valérie Clerc for putting us in touch. Without her, this book would never have existed.

We also want to thank the magnificent Ariana Museum for allowing us to take photographs on their premises.

Jan and Marie-José

* * *

My deepest appreciation to Caroline Thonger for our efficient and warm collaboration while working on the translation/ adaptation of this book.

My heartfelt gratitude to my friend Gabrielle for her constant help and encouragement over the years.

Marie-José

Introduction

My thirty years working in international circles have resulted in a startling realisation: other people recoil from working with us, the French. Managers hesitate before employing us, and colleagues from other cultures do their best to avoid us.

* * *

And yet there are so many aspects that visitors admire about France—much more that I could ever have imagined.

* * *

They love the diversity of the countryside—mountains from the Alps to the Pyrenees, the lavenders of Provence, the French Riviera, volcanoes, Evian water, the castles of the Dordogne and the chateaux of the Loire, the sophistication of Parisian monuments—an enormous variety within a relatively small country.

* * *

They are astounded by how our vines have been transplanted from Australia to California, passing via Argentina. They see us as alchemists or wizards in the technology of wine production, with an entire arcane vocabulary dedicated to wine-producing, and wine-tasting.

* * *

They appreciate the way we dress, and this is not only connected to 'haute couture', but also to the fact that something as simple as a pair of jeans can be worn with flair. Even the way we throw a scarf around our necks is regarded as stylish.

The highest veneration is accorded to our world-class cuisine, where we are recognised as the champions. Our Michelin Guide is a veritable Bible of gastronomy. Not only that, but even at the simplest level French food eaten in the family is guaranteed to taste good because the ingredients will have been picked out in the local market, with the bread bought daily in the local *boulangerie*.

* * *

Foreigners are astonished at the fact that we have more than 300 varieties of officially registered cheeses, and we can name them individually. We are proud to say that we have a different cheese for each day of the year.

* * *

What the rest of the world knows as a pie-chart, is called in French a *'camembert'*.

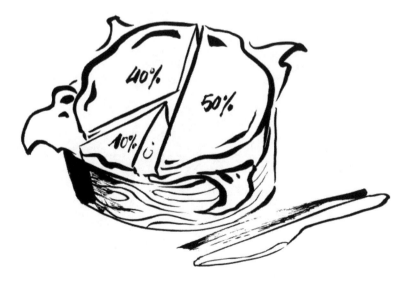

The French layperson has the reputation of being able to balance their cooking ingredients with an innately skillful touch—a pinch of herbs, a teaspoon of cream *et voilà*.

* * *

We are envied for being able to eat dishes swimming in cream and butter without putting on weight. The Americans use the expression 'French paradox' to describe this phenomenon. They have even conducted scientific experiments around this mystery. To date, however, they have not reached any explanation— neither have we, but why would we want to know?

* * *

All of this came as a great surprise to me. I had not expected that we French would be so praised and respected in all these spheres.

* * *

Then I began to pose the following question: how is it possible that we are so admired for the things we are not even conscious about, while being so condemned for personality traits that in my opinion are magnificent qualities?

How is it possible that:

our intense quest for justice is totally misunderstood and overlooked, and is even blamed for creating a negative atmosphere in a social and professional environment?

 our striving to attain intellectual excellence is considered as probing into matters too deeply?

 our sophisticated way of thinking is regarded as over-convoluted and liable to slow down the whole decision-making process?

 our brilliant talent for pointing out counter-arguments is interpreted as insolence or arrogance?

How is it possible that these qualities—that represent the very essence of our culture—are seen as flaws by the rest of the world?

* * *

The answer came to me as I was cooking a *gratin dauphinois*. There I stood poised, with the grater in one hand and a whole nutmeg in the other. I had to be very precise with the quantity to add to the dish. Too much, and it would all be spoiled. Not enough, and it would lack that essential flavour.

* * *

Achieving a successful recipe means being light-handed and balanced with the ingredients. As a French person, I am particularly aware of this. It's not too many cooks that spoil the broth, but too much of any single ingredient that will spoil the broth.

* * *

It suddenly dawned on me that this might be the reason why we French are perceived negatively by the rest of the world. We are doing things to excess!

* * *

Just as too much of any ingredient will spoil the taste of the dish, any personality trait used to excess might well spoil a relationship.

This stunning revelation brought me to a universal truth. Any quality will flip from positive to negative if flaunted to extreme.

* * *

For example, a surfeit of patience may result in lethargy; too much energy may create chaos and leave others behind; and over-organisation may transform a normal person into a control-freak.

* * *

This led me to explore the following hypothesis:

* * *

Could it be the excessive use of our good qualities that has given us the reputation for being so difficult?

* * *

I threw myself into a thorough investigation. And hereby I reveal some of my astonishing findings, under the following structure:

I will first introduce four fundamental elements of French culture:

The Spirit of the French Revolution

The Thirst for Culture

The Logic of Descartes

Contradiction as an Artform

Each chapter:

Identifies some specific character traits that constitute the essence of Frenchness.

* * *

Describes some qualities attached to each trait, highlighting their beauty and alerting you to the dangers of their excessive use.

* * *

Helps you overcome the challenge of reaching the perfect balance: just right and not too much.

* * *

Suggests some quick fixes that will allow you to turn the situation to your advantage.

* * *

I will then reveal the mystery of the Gallic cooking-pot,

* * *

And after a short journey through cultural differences,

* * *

I will bestow a touch of magic upon you, as a parting gift.

Four Elements of French Culture

1. The Spirit of the French Revolution
The birth of the Anti-Establishment Rebel

The French Revolution of 1789—that noted and noteworthy movement of popular expression—left its mark on the French collective psyche, and generated a people that excels at fighting against those in power.

The Revolutionary French

Since 1789 rebelliousness has always been a strong French trait. This is not taught as a subject at school—believe me—but it is nevertheless valued and encouraged in French children, at least insofar as questioning received opinion is concerned.

The outcome is that nowadays the French frequently find themselves clashing against the status quo. They feel that different sectors of society are entitled to protect their rights, and that it is the government's duty to meet the needs of the citizens.

This is why the French take to the streets and demonstrate so easily.

* * *

Foreign observers can only watch in amazement at the frequency of strikes in France, while most French citizens are remarkably tolerant of the disruption to their lives. What other option do they have, poor things?

Liberté, égalité, fraternité

Be compassionate, I implore all you non-French, about our situation. Our well-worn maxim *'liberté, égalité, fraternité'* has condemned us to living in Utopia, because our national emblem is in fact an impossible triangle.

* * *

Look, if I play loud music at night and disturb my neighbours, what's more important: exercising my personal freedom (liberty) or being a good neighbour/friend (fraternal)? If I help a friend with their job application form (being fraternal), is it not to the detriment of the other candidates (their equality)?

* * *

(Translator's note: The struggle is obvious, isn't it? Even interpreting these oh-so-French concepts into another language is an unending headache.)

Les gilets jaunes

This conundrum can be seen in the current crisis of the *gilets jaunes*.

* * *

It all started with French President Macron's decision to raise the tax on road fuel. A (supposedly) spontaneous movement arose against this through social media. People started gathering at roundabouts wearing their *gilets jaunes*—the symbol of vehicle drivers. In France it is compulsory to carry a *gilet jaune* (yellow vest) inside all vehicles driving on the road.

Very quickly this protest—restricted to fuel tax at first— degenerated into a form of grassroots revolt.

Every *gilet jaune* expressed their own particular gripe under the banner of *'liberté, égalité, fraternité'*, and started to voice their needs with statements such as: I want this, I have less than the other person, it's my right to ... It soon became apparent that these demands were as contradictory as they were irreconcilable.

* * *

Even the (very many) French who are opposed to the *gilet jaune* mentality, are themselves so conditioned by the same principle of *'liberté, égalité, fraternité'* that they are unable to voice their genuine dismay and consternation at the protesters.

* * *

What the French cannot prevent themselves from seeing is the legitimacy of each and every demand, no matter how disturbing.

* * *

Les insoumis

The element of rebelliousness has become entrenched into our DNA. We even have a political party called *'La France insoumise'*. The term *'insoumis'* means 'insubordinate' or 'going rogue'.

As the concept of democracy is based on the principle of majority rule, and everyone abiding by it, couldn't the naming of a political party as 'insubordinate' be by its very nature anti-democratic?

We want to believe that this party embodies a well-intended rebelliousness (a good quality), but isn't there the risk of it degenerating into potential chaos?

Some qualities of the revolutionary French—and where excess can lead us

• Our outbursts of anger give us the energy and strength to protect the vulnerable. This anger also serves as a mask to hide a whole range of emotions.

  When pushed to the extreme, this can make us look belligerent. We can even be labelled as insensitive to the feelings of others—an interpretation that is diametrically opposed to our original intention.

* * *

• We are so afraid of appearing ignorant, that we will do anything to defend our position and hide our lack of knowledge.

  When pushed to the extreme, this can make us reluctant to receive feedback and appear easily offended.

* * *

• Our ambivalent attitude towards authority prevents us from being too obedient and submitting to dictatorship.

  When pushed to the extreme this makes us appear moody and sulky.

To sum up

Our rebellious spirit can sometimes function like a centrifugal force—many a time our obsessive indignation turns round and round in our heads.

* * *

Look at how dictionaries have various definitions for the word *'revolution'*.
......*These include:*
- an abrupt and violent change in the political and social structure of a State, which happens when a group revolts against the authorities and takes over power
- the movement of an object around a central point or axis, periodically bringing it back to the same point.

(source: https://www.larousse.fr/dictionnaires/francais/révolution/69167)

* * *

Your overall challenge is:
to get us to evolve from *Revolution* to *Evolution*.

* * *

The word 'revolution' comprises both violent change and ... turning in circles. We are trapped in this paradox and can't even see it.

We French, revolutionaries to the very core, might well be motivated by a centrifugal force that prevents us from taking action.

* * *

You need to help us overcome this situation ... Please!

How can you succeed?

- I know it is hard for you, but when you engage us in conversation, have a go at being as indignant as we are— or at least pretend to be so.

* * *

- I know it's even harder, but congratulate us for wanting to save the world—even if you don't understand what we're on about.

* * *

- If we are boiling over, think of us as a bubbling cauldron. Don't put your hands in the pot, because you'll only get your fingers burnt. Just nod your head and leave us to cool down.

Three personality traits typical of the revolutionary mind and their quick fixes

• 1. Prone to anger

The French frequently express themselves in outbursts of temper. This has almost become an automatic reflex covering a whole gamut of emotions, such as:

being tired/exhausted; not being listened to/seen/recognised; frustration/powerlessness; sadness/disappointment; feeling accused/blamed/ignored; fear of ridicule/losing face; not being taken seriously.

By the way, these same emotions can also be hidden behind the apparently phlegmatic exterior of some other nations, can't they?

* * *

When anger is a positive tool

Anger is an extremely useful tool when it is a reaction to injustice. Anger generates energy, strength, and courage—or at least some kind of boldness.

Quick fix

When facing an angry French person, check for what's behind the reaction. If it's in defence of a just cause, then you can choose to take up the fight and/or offer additional ways of providing help. If it's for any other reason, simply breathe in and wait for the anger to dissipate.

* * *

In any case, don't ever think you can win against the French when we're angry; we'll always be better than you at letting off steam.

* * *

Keep your distance; don't take it personally; maintain your inner equilibrium.

But ... be careful. Don't be too zen on the outside—the French are allergic to it.

- **2. Easily offended**

We French hate being wrong or caught out. For us the expression "to put your head on the block" means risking ... the Guillotine.

* * *

So now you can easily understand why it is so hard for us to listen to a negative evaluation of our work, or to be told to change something in our behaviour. And this is why we sometimes react in a manner regarded by others as arrogant.

* * *

If you try to give us feedback by telling us we've made a mistake, you'll be met with a wall of resistance. Or worse, you will get the **boomerang effect.**

Quick fix

Rather than criticising us for what just happened, tell us how to achieve better results next time.

* * *

Think about providing **feed*forward*** (instead of feed*back).* Discuss what we could do better next time. Encourage us to envisage the future and potential positive outcomes.

And even better ... ask us for our opinion!

* * *

If you ask a French person for their opinion or point of view, you will surely get this, and in spades.

Make us express aloud what can be done, and we will be caught out at our own game. Not only will we love doing it but we will feel in control, and this is surely the best way to have us on board.

- **3. Ambivalent towards authority**

The French have a very ambiguous relationship with power and hierarchy. Professional, social or intellectual 'success' attracts them as much as it makes them feel ill-at-ease.

* * *

They have a tendency to put their 'superiors' on a pedestal, while at the same time feeling rebellious against them.
In fact, bosses (and aristocrats) are at once reviled and revered.

* * *

As soon as the French find themselves within a hierarchical structure, they tend to believe that responsibility lies entirely on the shoulders of the boss or chief—whether for effective institutional decisions or for successful social interactions.

* * *

The French are apt to place all bosses into the same basket, irrespective of their individual differences. Their status is viewed with an element of distrust.

* * *

Furthermore, building professional relationships, or making use of networking is a problem for the French. To benefit from any sort of privilege is regarded as taboo. A person graduating from one of the prestigious 'Grandes Ecoles' will be despised as belonging to an unapproachable clique, while at the same time being covertly respected and admired (in the same way as bosses and aristocrats).

Quick fix

If you are the boss, make your French employees aware of their importance in their particular sphere of responsibility. Tell them honestly how well they are doing, and you will create a different set of dynamics between employer and employee.

* * *

Make it clear that the decision-making process belongs to you, but that at the same time, in your human interactions, each person has the same power and influence irrespective of their grade or position.

* * *

If a French employee is closed off, take this as totally normal behaviour. Let them sulk for a moment; don't pay too much attention.

* * *

When deserved, give them a praise for specific behaviours.

* * *

Avoid flattery like "You're great", but instead use comments such as:

......"I really appreciate the accuracy of the figures you gave me yesterday."

......"I like the way you interact with our pool of consultants."

2. The Thirst for Culture
......The Age of Enlightenment

The Age of Enlightenment spread throughout Europe during the seventeenth and eighteenth centuries.

The Cultured French

For us French, the Age of Enlightenment has remained a pivotal moment in history. We remember it mostly as a literary movement that started in 1715 and ended with the French Revolution in 1789.

For the rest of the world, the Age of Enlightenment covered a broader period beginning in 1620 and ending in 1789. (source: New World Encyclopedia).

* * *

It also looks as if most nations remember this movement in a greater diversity of areas including the sciences.

* * *

For the English, as an example, this is still regarded as the start of a scientific revolution, with the veneration of polymaths such as Newton and other scientists studying mathematics, astronomy, chemistry and medicine. It also encompasses the creation of the Royal Society for the propagation of the sciences.

* * *

For the French, the Age of Enlightenment is mainly connected to philosophers and writers, such as Voltaire, Diderot, Montesquieu. And these giants of Literature and Philosophy have passed into posterity and have remained dominant reference points.

* * *

The wisdom of these outstanding intellects weighs heavily upon the French today, in the same way that an illustrious ancestor could be both a model and a heavy burden for the descendants.

* * *

Have pity on today's poor little schoolchildren having to cope with a system still based on eighteenth-century philosophy. This also applies, to a certain extent, to other French-speaking countries such as Switzerland and Belgium, and even spreads further to the former French colonies.

* * *

Acquiring colonies was not merely a question of economics for us French. There was also an instinctive necessity to expand French culture throughout the world, including literature, history and philosophy.

* * *

Local children in the remotest corners of Africa were not only taught to read and write in French, but also had to learn by heart the fact that their ancestors were ... Gauls!

The Académie Française

The sole objective of the *Académie Française*, that world-famous institution, is the defence—meaning the standardisation and perfection—of the French language.

* * *

Members of the *Académie Française* are considered to be like the immortal gods, officially titled *'les Immortels'*. They are appointed for life. They are all highly regarded published authors, thinkers and philosophers. A major aspect of their work is their commitment to excellence, especially in the written form of the French language.

* * *

The *Académie* comprises 40 members. One of them has to die before the next one is elected by their peers. This is such a complex and politically sensitive process, presently there are four vacant seats out of the 40. The remaining 36 members cannot agree on who should be nominated among the many applicants.

* * *

Being elected as an *'immortel'* is considered as the pinnacle of French cultural achievement. The *Académie* is the only institution in French society whose members still wear an exclusively designed outfit, consisting of highly-embroidered jacket and tailored trousers, and including a sword.

* * *

The standardization of the French language by the *Académie* is not without problems nowadays. Many Francophone countries can't decide whether they should follow the norms of the *Académie* or not. At the same time, none of them have yet gone as far as creating their own version of the *Académie*.

Les 'intellectuels'

While the *Académie Française* represents the tradition of French language and literature, in more recent times waves of new concepts and new ways of thinking have emerged. One of the best examples is existentialism, which arose in the 50s and 60s after the Liberation of France, with Jean-Paul Sartre as the standard-bearer.

* * *

This spontaneous movement, born amid the cigarette smoke of the cafés on the Rive Gauche in Paris, encompassed the essence of controversy as well as elements of the rebellious spirit of the French.

* * *

Writers such as Sartre, Gide and de Beauvoir promoted new ways of thinking. At the same time is has to be noted that they adhered to the conventional standards of the French language. They were challenging societal norms, but abiding by linguistic norms.

* * *

From that point onwards, the denomination of *'les intellectuels'* was created in French culture. It refers to a highly-regarded and slightly feared caste in French society. The term *'intellectuel'* applies only to those interested in literature and philosophy. This concept has nothing to do with being a member of a club or institution, but is more like some sort of honorific title mysteriously bestowed by the media or academic circles.

* * *

Strange to tell, this has been totally accepted by French society in general. In essence, we French—normally prepared to argue about anything and everything—are so impressed by our culture and by the very concept of *'intellectuels'*, that as soon as we come face to face with a creature supposedly belonging to this elite group we bow down before them in fear and humility.

Some qualities of the cultured French—and where excess can lead us

- Our great need for in-depth knowledge makes us delve beneath the surface of a subject and probe until we find unexpected answers or solutions.

  When pushed to the extreme, this means we might get bogged in details and not be structured enough.

* * *

- Our quest for transparency prevents us from being led by the nose and from following potentially wrong paths.

  When pushed to the extreme, this can make us suspicious and inquisitive, chronically suspecting others of hiding things from us.

* * *

- We expect a lot from ourselves, and this drives us towards excellence and away from mediocrity.

  When pushed to the extreme, this makes us appear arrogant or demanding when in fact we are lost in self-doubt.

To sum up

Being immersed in tiny details and reams of documents, we miss the broad view. In fact, sometimes we can't even see the forest for the trees.

* * *

We would truly gain a lot by expanding our field of vision and working on what the Americans call 'the big picture'.

* * *

We shouldn't forget that the inventors of the moving picture, the cinema, were *'les Frères Lumière'*, two brothers from Lyon (by the way, one of the most renowned cities for its gastronomy).

Your overall challenge is:

to help us to gain perspective—pull us up from the depths of knowledge to the heights of a 360° bird's-eye view

* * *

All we need is to get rid of our dark thoughts and shine the spotlight onto life in the 21st century.

How can you succeed?

- Value our knowledge, the richness of our language.
  Congratulate us for the vast vocabulary relating to food
  and wine, a wonderful source of inspiration.

* * *

- When you talk to us and you feel the need to beat us at
  our own intellectual game, use literary references such as
  Shakespeare.
  We are so respectful and ignorant of the Bard, and
  other authors like him, that any such mention will stun
  us into momentary silence.

* * *

- Refer to British traditions.
  Despite our loathing of royalty in general, we French
  love the pomp and ceremony (and scandals) of the
  British Royal Family.

Three personality traits typical of the cultured mind and their quick fixes

- ## 1. Lacking structure

Have you ever experienced a meeting with French people? It is difficult for us to fit the intricacy of our ideas into a simple and clear framework. Obviously, by contradicting ourselves we often lose sight of the ultimate goal.

* * *

Although perfectly aware of this tendency, and kicking ourselves after every meeting, we nevertheless repeat the pattern.

* * *

We French consider any attempt to impose rules of procedure on a meeting as too authoritarian. This can often create a free-for-all, letting the meeting run on for much longer than necessary and failing to reach any conclusion. While we all complain about this, nobody actually manages to change the situation.

Quick fix

- Help us understand that setting up a strict framework is an excellent and effective way of allowing everyone to put forward their point of view. It will not take us long to grasp that if the meeting is chaired firmly but fairly, everyone will have to express themselves and be heard.

* * *

- Create roles for each member: chair, timekeeper, note-taker, etc. Be polite but firm when you give the floor. We will grumble at first, but by the end we will have seen the benefits. And you need to believe me, because I don't think any of my compatriots will ever admit this to your face.

* * *

- Show us that not all structures have to be a vertical hierarchy—they can also be horizontal. This will allow us to express our complex ideas without us needing to be forceful.

* * *

- Give us some space (at the end maybe) in which we can argue. Value the controversy ... to a certain extent.

2. Being suspicious

Our philosophical and intellectual approach, combined with our tendency to go deeply into matters (see the previous Chapter), leads us to seek the rationale behind every situation.

Our most renowned French detective, Maigret, builds his entire investigation on delving into the darkest corners of the human psyche, and he's very successful at solving the problem by using this method.

* * *

We plunge into the very nub of problems and then look into the why, the how, the who, the when ... in fact we apply a philosophical analysis to every aspect of our lives. This is an exhausting process, believe me. If you succeed in lifting even part of this burden the benefits will become immediately apparent for all the parties involved—but it is really not easy.

* * *

In the workplace, we tend to question every statement, motivation or reasoning of our bosses.

Quick fix

- **In the workplace**

Clarify the limit of what you can share. Beyond a certain point, matters become confidential and cannot be shared with others. If you are submitted to intrusive questioning, cut it off by stating clearly: "I'm not answering this," and then walk away to prevent any possibility of further discussion.

* * *

- **In personal relationships**

Use the iceberg as a metaphor for your whole personality. The 10% showing above the surface is what you want to show to the world. The 90% hidden below the water represents your fundamental values, secret desires, unconscious needs and so on. Nobody is allowed to even approach this part, unless you give them specific and voluntary permission to do so.

If you feel someone is questioning your motives, or making comments about your personality, ask them to describe the specific behaviour or action they expect from you. Decide whether you are willing to implement it or not.

* * *

Example:

Comment: "Oh, you're always in such a hurry, Mary."
Response: "Where do you need me to slow down, in order for us to work together on this project in the best possible way?"

3. Self-doubting

In the French education system, it's very rare for the teachers to give schoolchildren a higher mark than 13/20 (the UK equivalent of a B-). The American school system of awarding 'straight A's' is unthinkable in France.

* * *

American students often need to spend a year abroad as part of their graduate studies. Many of them will avoid France because they find the marking system so discouraging. With the same results in another country they would be rated much higher, something of great importance to them because those grades form part of their degree.

* * *

I'll let you in on a secret: our flamboyant exterior actually conceals a poor little being racked with self-doubt. The benchmark of the great philosophers is so impossible to attain that we feel humbled, belittled and unworthy. Thus, we become insecure and it is difficult for us to hold our heads high in the international arena.

Quick fix

Being in a situation where we might need to admit our ignorance, places us in a state of panic. This is when we flaunt our peacock tails to hide our flaws, an attitude that might be interpreted as us being too proud of ourselves, or snobbish.

Now you understand that instead of being annoyed at our apparent display of ego, you should comfort us and reassure us.

* * *

Value our knowledge and contribution. We rarely receive compliments or encouragement.

Test it out, and the outcome could be a real surprise—both for you and for your counterpart.

* * *

Anecdote

In 2004, my 14-year-old son and I moved to the States. My son attended an American High School, even though his knowledge of English was somewhat sketchy.

The first weeks went by without incident, until I received a phone call one evening from the school secretary, summoning me to an interview with the Principal.

I have to admit that my son's scholastic path up to that point hadn't been the smoothest, so when I found myself sitting with him in front of no less than THREE teachers and the Principal, I feared the worst. The Principal's subsequent pronouncement, however, left me flabbergasted.

"We wanted to inform you of your son's excellent integration into the school, to congratulate him for his hard work and to encourage him to continue in the same vein."

It's impossible to describe how dumbfounded my son and I were to to receive such compliments. In France, to be called up by the school would only mean trouble.

After this, my son gained in confidence throughout his academic career, even after his return to France.

I sometimes wonder whether the glittering path he then followed in his studies could be partly credited to the Principal of Irvington High School. *Merci, Monsieur!*

Language skills
'British' English and the French language—an *entente cordiale*?

A new-born child can hear sounds within the range of 20 to 20,000 Hertz. But the infant brain then focuses on the sounds required by its mother tongue. Some languages cover a broad range of sounds: Russian and the Scandinavian tongues use frequencies from 125 to 8,000 Hertz, which partially explains why we find those nations to be 'good at languages'.

* * *

The French language, in contrast, uses the range of 125 to 2,000 Hertz, whereas 'British' English uses 2,000 to 12,000 Hertz—the overlap between the two languages being very narrow. This is an indication of the tiny window of communication between the two nations.

* * *

A rough representation of these discrepancies is shown in the graph below, ranging from 125 to 12,000 Hz.

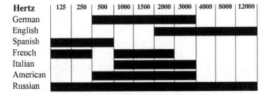

As French ears are unaccustomed to the range of frequencies used by the English language—and ... vice versa—each nation struggles as much as the other to distinguish the sounds they use.

* * *

This goes a long way to explain why we French find it so difficult to understand spoken 'British' English, whereas it is easier for us to converse with an American (at least in terms of wavelength).

3. The Logic of Descartes:
......An Unending Thinking Process

René Descartes is known the world over, and to this day the French are famous for their Cartesian logic.

The Logical French

The French have a way of reasoning based on the logic of Descartes. This can turn into an unending thinking process which goes something like this:

* * *

- put forward a hypothesis
- test it out by imagining the consequences
- take another hypothesis
- test it out by imagining the consequences
- take another hypothesis ... *ad infinitum*

This way of reasoning is perfectly applicable to any kind of scientific endeavour, and Descartes was a man of science. In the 17th century, he considered that life was divided into three distinct areas: Medicine, Method (or Sciences), and Morality.

* * *

He applied his method of reasoning to each area in more or less the same way, because at that point in history, Morality was strictly coded by religion and society.

Moral constraints are much less severe today, and religion—certainly in France—no longer plays such a pivotal role.

* * *

The astonishing fact is that for the French, Descartes is mostly known as a philosophical thinker. The other aspects of his knowledge are rarely brought into the debate.

* * *

When the scientific approach to reasoning is applied to contemporary moral themes, the process will go round and round in endless circles (hypothesis-1, development-1, impossible conclusion-1; hypothesis-2, development-2, impossible conclusion; and so on).

* * *

When this way of thinking extends to social interactions, or to taking everyday decisions in the professional or personal sphere, the number of hypotheses to consider is infinite. It then becomes difficult to take any final decisions.

* * *

It is such a burden to consider every aspect of a problem and never be able to reach a conclusion, that it becomes discouraging.

* * *

That is why the French suffer from a little voice at the back of their heads. And it never says: "you're so brilliant", "everything's fine", "you deserve the best in life".

* * *

Quite the contrary! The nagging little demon inside us does nothing but badger us with phrases such as: "You're making the same mistake again" / "You're being too ambitious, who d'you think you are?" / "The world is a bad place / stop kidding yourself" — each message more crushing than the last.

* * *

I know that most people, wherever they live on the planet, have a similar small voice in their heads. For some reason — maybe because it's a wine-lover and gourmet — this seems to be particularly attached to us French. And it has managed to transform us into a nation of chronic pessimists.

Neuroticism

Anecdote

During a recent conference, a psychiatrist offered the following definition of psychosis versus neurosis: "The neurotic is painfully aware of their illness and has an acute sense of reality — but is not looking for treatment. The psychotic is unaware of their illness and has lost contact with reality."

A Frenchman next to me joked: "This defines us French very well."

Faced with my expression of surprise, he continued: "The psychotic thinks that two plus two equals five and is perfectly happy in that belief. The neurotic knows that two plus two equals four, and hates it. Don't you think this is the very definition of us French — a neurotic nation confronted by a psychotic rest of the world?"

* * *

This remark demonstrates how we French wallow in melancholia, and that we have not the slightest interest in searching for a cure.

Pessimism and grammar

Even our use of grammar highlights our inclination towards pessimism.

* * *

We often express ourselves with the past conditional tense. Revisiting the past is one sure-fire way of plunging yourself into depression.

* * *

We love using phrases such as: « *Ah si seulement j'avais su, j'aurais ...* »

(Oh, if only I had known, I could have/I would have). And of course we visualise beautiful outcomes that would probably never have happened and make our current situation seem miserable.

* * *

oui / si
We often ask questions in the negative form.

* * *

For example, an English proposal would go:
......"What about the cinema tonight?"
A French person would say:
......"*Tu ne viendrais pas au cinéma avec moi ce soir?*"
......Wouldn't you like to come out to the cinema tonight?

* * *

We have even created a special word to be able to give a positive answer to a negative question. Amongst all the Latin languages, French is the only one to have two words to express a positive answer to a request:

* * *

- One is *'oui'*. We use 'oui' to give a positive response to an open question
  Tu aimes le fromage ? Oui
......Do you like cheese? Yes
- One is *'si'*. We use 'si' to give a positive response to a negative question.
  ......*Tu n'aimes pas le fromage ? Si* (or even, *'mais si'*)
......You don't like cheese, do you? Yes, I do (or, of course I do)

* * *

If we go back to the first example about the cinema, there could be two possible replies:
......*"Tu ne viendrais pas au cinéma avec moi ce soir?"*
......*"Si, avec plaisir."*
......Wouldn't you like to come out to the cinema tonight?
......Sure, I'd love to.

* * *

Another reply could also be:
......*"Tu ne viendrais pas au cinéma avec moi ce soir?"*
......*"Non, merci."*
......Wouldn't you like to come out to the cinema tonight?
......No thank you.

Hexagon

The French media often refer to the French nation as a hexagon, because of the shape of the country.

Maybe this creates a feeling of being locked inside a box. Consequently, don't ever approach us French with the concept of 'thinking outside the box' — how we dislike all Americanised clichés, and this one more than all of them.

Some qualities of the logical French—and where excess can lead us

- We excel at evaluating risks and identifying problems, and it's a real asset to be cautious especially faced with any major transition.

  When this is pushed to the extreme, this will make us appear totally resistant to change.

* * *

- Our complex way of thinking demonstrates our innate ability to find the connections between ideas and link them together, sometimes in the most intricate ways.

  When pushed to the extreme, this might make others feel that we are indecisive and that we create an impasse.

* * *

- We find lots of counter-arguments, and this is an excellent way of exploring a whole array of solutions.

  When pushed to the extreme, this can be considered as a defensive attitude.

To sum up

We are so well-trained in thinking complex thoughts that it has become totally natural to do so. We are so proud of this achievement that we use it extensively.

* * *

To express the act of thinking, we have two words in French: *penser* (think) and *réflechir* (reflect), the second one being used far more frequently than the first one and in the most trivial of situations. *Want to go to the movies tonight? I'll reflect about it* (instead of 'I'll think about it').

* * *

This business of discussing the cinema in France (or anything else, for that matter) can drive you really mad, can't it?

Your overall challenge is:
to prevent us from reflecting too much

* * *

The cat's-eye embedded in a road does not have its own source of light, but only reflects the light that shines upon it from a vehicle's headlights. This, you'll agree, is very useful for delineating the edges of a space. It cannot, however, light up the path.

* * *

Being so keen on this concept of reflection in our thinking process, we might be faced with the same limitation. We are so focused on the thinking process, that it fails to offer any illumination.

How can you succeed?

To keep the peace (or at least not make enemies of us), tell us how open you are to listening (and remember that listening doesn't mean agreeing) to the objections we are raising.

* * *

When interacting with us, be firm as soon as we begin prevaricating. Make us get out of our heads and look outside.

* * *

If you cannot involve us in the decision-making process, then take it out of our hands and make the decision for us.

Three personality traits typical of the logical mind and their quick fixes

• 1: Opposed to change

We are good at visualising future obstacles, and expert in extensively analysing the current situation. As soon as any kind of change is mentioned, our system goes into overdrive. We become immediately conscious of everything we could lose, and of the potential dangers. We then convince ourselves that the new situation could be much worse than the existing one.

This is why we have the reputation for being resistant to change.

* * *

The reality is that very often we prevent others from getting rid of things that could still be very useful.

Quick fix

On the one hand, if you are a project manager or risk manager make sure to hire a French person (maybe two would be too many) with the specific task of evaluating risks, losses, obstacles, problems. In every category of risk assessment, the French are the champions.

* * *

On the other hand, if you work with employees who demonstrate a resistance to change, then value their attitude. Their desire to stick with a situation shows how attached they are to what they have. Nobody will move on to new ideas if they feel that everything they have achieved up to that point will be erased.

* * *

The tendency in many of today's companies to push for rapid change is in fact often counter-productive, because of the feeling by many employees that management has failed to recognise their accomplishments.

* * *

Praise and thank your staff for expressing an attachment to the past. You can even organise a party to celebrate the past.

- **2: Indecisive**

Our French minds have been shaped by René Descartes, and spiralling from one thought to the next is our way of thinking.

* * *

No need to discuss this further! The obvious conclusion is that we need help in coming to any sort of decision.

* * *

We are so terrified of making the wrong choice that when placed in a situation where we need to choose, we might react defensively. Don't panic if you find yourself on the receiving end of a possible outburst of anger. Bear with us.

* * *

You non-French believe that getting something done is better than getting it perfect. This concept is incomprehensible to us French. We're obsessed by the idea that whatever we do will never be perfect, and that prevents us from taking action.

* * *

Our difficulty in reaching decisions even applies to the French justice system. France as a nation has been condemned on various occasions by the European Court in Strasbourg, for the excessive delays in the judicial process. Our lengthy process could partly be due to a lack of resources, but at the same time there is most likely an inherent lack of will to solve the problem.

Quick fix

If you sense us getting close to the 'reflective effect', and that this might result in problems such as slowing down or blocking the decision-making process, then ...

* * *

Use distractions.
Get us busy, offer us a coffee, interest us in a conversation, do what you can—anything to avoid us getting tangled up in our thoughts.

* * *

If this doesn't work, then listen to us and take note of all our ideas, to reassure us that they won't be lost. Then slowly take us by the hand and make us understand that:

- there is a cost to making a choice
- choosing means giving up something else
- no solution is perfect
- freedom is a complex thing—and downright cruel!
- the future might prove us right, or perhaps not
- in any case, you won't be chastised.

* * *

And if we are brave enough to make a choice...
don't forget to congratulate us.

- **3. Defensive**

Even if the French have in essence retained the philosophical aspect of hypothetical deductive reasoning proposed by Descartes, there is a strong scientific element at its root.

* * *

When a scientific experiment is carried out using this model, the outcome will be right or wrong, true or false.

* * *

We French tend to apply this scientific reasoning to human interactions. We therefore seek for proof that statements can only be wrong or right, false or true. The reality is that in interpersonal relationships, this is rarely the case. In most situations, all points of view need to be considered as being potentially valid, or acknowledged as such.

Watch out: at the back of their minds, the French tend to hold the belief that if one person is right, then the other person must be wrong. This can affect the way we approach a conversation.

Quick fix

Now that you're aware of the scientific reasons behind our defensive and outspoken attitude, you no longer have to take it personally.

On the contrary.

* * *

- Encourage us to take part in a discussion, value our contributions for the sake of them (even if the proposal is unsuitable).

* * *

- Paraphrase what we have just said, and make us clarify our statements if they are a bit woolly.

* * *

- Tell a French person: "That's a good idea", and they will be your friend for life.

* * *

It's so unusual for us to receive compliments! Not that our compatriots are bad friends, but they are exercising their exceptional skills searching for the errors in our reasoning and deciding who is wrong or right.

Body language

The typical image of a French person includes:

- unsynchronised and un-parallel movements
- shrugging the shoulders
- the body bending forwards instead of remaining upright
- elbows leaning on surfaces
- making a sort of 'pfft' noise to indicate doubt
- rising intonation at the end of sentences (even when making statements).

These gestures can be interpreted as defensive, but couldn't they also be the sign of a lack of self-confidence and assertiveness? I leave it up to you to decide.

Finding solutions

While I struggled with this chapter, I found the following artwork on the Internet:

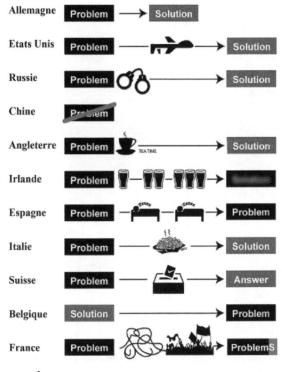

@jeromevadon

* * *

Somehow, I found it 'politically incorrect', and at the same time, I couldn't help bursting out laughing.

* * *

Flags listed: Germany, USA, Russia, China, UK, Ireland, Spain, Italy, Switzerland, Belgium, France

4 – Contradiction as an Artform
......The Essay: Mission Impossible

In the French education system, all schoolchildren from the age of 16 are obliged to take Philosophy as one of their main subjects, irrespective of their choices in the field of the arts or the sciences. This means they all have to write essays in preparation for the Baccalaureate.

The contradictory French

We French have the reputation of being contradictory, something I find astonishing. I have always understood that other countries have other customs, but it never occurred to me that this particular trait of having a contradictory mind was so developed in us compared with the rest of the world.

* * *

It took me a while to realise that most people have an adverse reaction to this contradictory attitude, and even longer to understand why. It goes without saying that I have modified my approach and taken some of this on board (otherwise I would never have undertaken to write this book). Now, will I ever reach the point where it comes naturally? Hmm, maybe one day.

Searching for the causes of this situation has been one of the most perplexing problems I have faced. The solution jumped out at me one day while I was tidying up some old school papers. I came across a pile of compositions. Leafing through the numerous pages, I noticed that they were liberally laced with hundreds of 'nevertheless', 'on the other hand', 'however', 'on the contrary' and 'but ... but ... but'.

* * *

In other words, essays written in school contain lists and lists of objections. What a shock! This was something I had never realised before: from early childhood our minds are shaped to become the wizards of contradiction.

The essay

The French essay is based on Plato's dialectical method.

* * *

According to Wikipedia:
the dialectical method is at base a discourse between two or more
people holding different points of view about a subject but wishing
to convince the other of their point of view through reasoned
arguments.

* * *

Philosophy courses are designed to lead students to develop
their own opinions and teach them how to present them in the
most coherent and effective way.

* * *

An essay follows strict rules: the students are given a statement
in the form of an affirmation or a question.

- In the first section of their essay, the students write down
  a few general ideas and jot down some references to the
  great Philosophers.
- In the second much longer section the students present
  their own point of view. And, oddly enough, this must be
  expressed in the form of ... counter-arguments!

* * *

Consequently, in the first section, the students must demonstrate that they have absorbed the sacred writings of the grand masters.

* * *

Most importantly, in the second section, the students have to express their **own unique points of view**. These must be original, relevant, unexpected, imaginative … and they have to be presented in the form of counter-arguments.

* * *

This objective is almost mission impossible, considering that the students' own points of view are competing with those of the grand masters of literature and philosophy—and yet this is exactly what we are trained to achieve.

* * *

Philosophy essays are produced with the sweat of our brow. They are expected to be four to six pages long; we spend four hours on a single topic; we dig into our deepest cultural references; and we strive to generate original ideas. Our ultimate goal being nothing less than to surpass and contradict (!) the theories of the grand masters.

* * *

It is as simple as that. The source of the contradictory spirit of the French stems from the fact that from adolescence onward, we are moulded to give the best of ourselves through opposition and contradiction.

Beyond borders

The contradictory mind goes beyond the French geographical borders to include the entire French-speaking world. We have coined a word for this: '*Francophonie*', as if it were an independent mythical planet like Atlantis, or Oceania in Aldous Huxley's 'Brave New World'.

* * *

Anecdote

In an international organisation, two identical training courses were held in English and in French. The courses were led by the same trainers: one was of Romanian origin, the other Swiss-German. Neither trainer had English or French as their native language.

As for the participants in the courses delivered in French, they were a mix of French native speakers (a few of them French nationals, but most of them from other French-speaking countries: Belgium, Luxembourg, Benin, Côte d'Ivoire). And some of them were non-native French speakers but fluent in French.

The same applied to the participants attending the courses delivered in English. It included native speakers from Australia, the US, the UK and non-native English speakers fluent in English.

In summary, in both cases they came from all over the world and had chosen the language that was the easiest for them.

Both trainers taught the same content. And the courses were delivered about ten times in each language to different groups.

At the end of each course, evaluations assessing the content of the course and the teaching skills of the trainer were completed and returned. Strangely enough, the marks were very different between the two groups. The English-speaking participants gave an average mark of 4.8/5 whereas the mark from the French-speaking participants barely averaged 4/5.

* * *

As organisers of these repeated courses, we tried to analyse these differences. We were unable to find any logical factor behind them. We could only come up with the hypothesis that it was the use of the French language that made the participants more critical ...

Some qualities of the contradictory French—and where excess can lead us

- As soon as an idea becomes popular, we are immediately able to see its many threads, shortcomings and passing fads. This saves time and energy in the long run.

    When pushed to the extreme, this makes us seem negative and critical

* * *

- Every time an idea is put forward, it's a real game for us to enter into an intellectual competition. The beauty of this is that it generates new ways of thinking and opens up possibilities.

When pushed to the extreme, this might appear provocative.

* * *

- If a new project is on the drawing board, our capacity to search for inconsistencies will help the group ensure that everything is well-aligned

    When pushed to the extreme, this will bar us from being real contributors and from putting forward suggestions.

To sum up

Our readiness to present counter-arguments can create an atmosphere of conflict rather than cooperation.

We are so focused on the end result that sometimes we do not consider the feelings of others or the impact of our remarks on them.

* * *

It would be such an advantage if we could finally reveal our soft underbelly to the world. We would then become as generous in our relationships as we are when entertaining guests at home around our perfectly prepared meal ...

* * *

Easier said than done, perhaps, but at least we could give it a go.

Your overall challenge is:
to get us knitting relationships and weaving ideas together

We are so obsessed with the ideas inside our heads, that when we express them out loud we forget to consider the effect they might have on other people's feelings.

* * *

Help us untangle our complex ball of ideas, and knit relationships with other people. In this way, we will be able to put ideas together and weave them into a cohesive and comforting piece of fabric.

* * *

Furthermore, knitting is an activity that has a soothing and calming effect. This could even make us less excitable.

How can you succeed?

* Compliment us, reassure us, and give us good marks.

* * *

* Listen to our point of view even if we have cut you off.
    We French are not very good at listening to what the
    other person is saying because, from the first minute
    of a conversation, we are busy preparing counter-
    arguments.

* * *

* Take the time to paraphrase or repeat back to us what we
    have just said.
    You cannot be heard if the other person thinks they
    have not been heard. This is a general rule that applies
    in particular to the French.

* * *

* Help us identify our talents.
    We are the first victims of our critical minds. Being
    harsh critics applies first and foremost ... to ourselves.
    Not only can we see the faults in others; most of all we
    see them in ourselves.
    We are so used to being 'average' in education, and to
    using expressions like *'pas mal'* (not too bad) to mean
    that something is 'really good', that we find it almost
    impossible to recognise our own talents.

Help us to highlight the times when we have:

done something more than planned/more than others/more than asked of us

* * *

- done something differently

* * *

- done something without having to

* * *

- done something with less (saving on resources)

* * *

- avoided doing something, while achieving a satisfactory outcome.

* * *

Remember the universal rule: the higher your level of self-confidence, the lower your level of tension and hostility.

* * *

Do whatever you can to boost the level of self-confidence of your French counterparts—and this might dramatically improve the relationship.

Identifying the USP

Rather than seeking to eradicate the differences in us French, uncover our Unique Selling Proposition (and use it for your own benefit!).

* * *

The USP is a marketing formula used to find a particular product's distinguishing features, showing how it stands out from the competition and making it unique.

* * *

Sit with us, and encourage us to talk about the elements that make us unique or different from everybody else: professional experience, studies, travel, clubs, leisure pursuits, cultural tastes, sports, etc.

* * *

Make us become conscious of all our accomplishments, and let us dream for a while.

You might dislike feel-good gimmicks, but give this one a try and let yourself be surprised by the outcome.

Three personality traits typical of the contradictory mind and their quick fixes

* * *

- **1. Critical**

Being critical is regarded as one of most unpleasant characteristics of the French. Most people do not appreciate being on the receiving end of a series of 'but ... but ... but'.

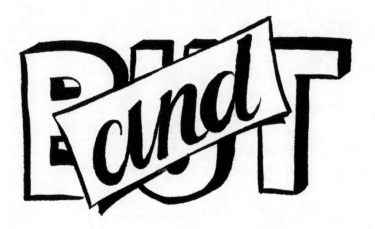

As seen in the Introduction, our minds have been shaped by years of strict academic training in the craftsmanship of contradiction.

* * *

It is true that 'but' is one of our favourite words, and it has a number of 'clever cousins' such as 'however', 'although', 'nevertheless', 'on the other hand', and so on. These are the standard-bearers of the objection, the banners of the counter-argument.

Quick fix

As soon as you hear a French person using 'but' in a sentence, make a mental note of it. Remember that when a French person objects, they are giving the best of themselves. Try and forget your feeling of being rejected, and grasp the substance of the information because it might be where the most interesting nuggets are to be found.

Criticism and creativity
Anecdote

While I was writing this book, every French person that I consulted for feedback threw up dozens of objections and specific counter-arguments.

To be honest, the objections were perfectly valid. By putting my ego and impatience to one side, I was able to take them on board. I reached the point, however, when this became counter-productive—there was a surfeit of negativity and too little encouragement.

In order to know which elements of the book were any good, I turned to my foreign friends. I then received a much broader range of comments, from suggesting changes to providing positive reinforcement.

If I had not received the negative feedback from the French, I might have kept my head in the clouds and not been critical enough on myself. If I had nothing but that, I might quite possibly have given up.

* * *

This is a typical example of the effects of the critical mind pushed to extreme.

- **2 : Provocative**

Anecdote

Fresh out of one of the French *Grandes Ecoles* (elite schools), a young executive confessed rather gleefully: "When I come out of a meeting where everyone's in agreement, I'm not happy. The only way to make progress is to have a bit of 'argy-bargy'."

Two months later, utterly dismayed, he complained of having the unions on his back and how hostile they were being.

When he was reminded of his love for 'argy-bargy' in his meetings, he was taken aback, explaining in all good faith that this was 'just a game' for him, a thrilling intellectual exercise—a total delight, and even a brain-massage.

* * *

This story is self-explanatory. It demonstrates that there can be an element of delight and intellectual playfulness behind some attitudes that others would consider provocative.

Quick fix

In some countries people get a buzz from jogging, others from drinking tea, whereas we French find our greatest pleasure in being involved in controversy.

* * *

Don't be overwhelmed by our outspoken nature. Being provocative is one of our national sports—in fact, it has an element of fun for us.

* * *

We are always happy when we can find a sparring partner. Be a good sport and play with us for a while. We adore verbal jousting so much that we practise it at every opportunity: in private, amongst friends, in the professional context and in public on TV.

* * *

As a matter of fact, such confrontations are not restricted to political discussions but extend to interviews and round tables— whether in the sphere of literature, the arts, music, variety shows and other artistic activities.

The Americans make jokes on the "Late-Night Show", enthuse about Oprah Winfrey, and congratulate each other on the Ellen de Generes show. Even when politicians are invited, the atmosphere remains friendly.

* * *

Equivalent French programmes featuring guests such as artists, comedians, film directors, writers or sports personalities, are often designed to generate controversy.

* * *

......We have a very popular TV show called '*Salut les terriens*' (greetings Earthlings) on Saturdays and Sundays. The main presenter, Thierry Ardisson, is accompanied by seven commentators that he calls his 'mercenaries', whose role is to torture the guests with tricky, inquisitive and invasive questions.

* * *

......In another very popular show, '*On n'est pas couché*' (we're not in bed yet), the presenter makes the guest sit alone in the middle of a circle, and releases two commentators with ferocious reputations onto them (one right-wing, one left-wing), when in fact the guests are not from the political arena. Far from it—most of them are drawn from the cinema or popular culture.

The huge audience figures confirm how much we French love this modern-day version of the Roman circuses. And not only do we love watching these shows—each of us is secretly dreaming of taking part, to prove our prowess at witty repartee.

- **3. Hesitant at making suggestions**

Anecdote

In my first months as a trainer in an international organisation, I could often be found raising objections or pointing out shortcomings during the meetings.

Instead of praising my contributions, my boss at the time—an authoritarian and impatient Anglo-Jamaican woman—used to ask me with a long-suffering sigh, "So what do you suggest?".

......I was taken aback and annoyed by these brusque requests, and it took me several weeks to swallow my resentment.

Determined to take up my rightful place with these new duties, and to be recognised for my true worth, I started doing what was expected of me: coming up with suggestions.

* * *

To my great surprise (because I had ended up thinking that my co-workers and my boss "didn't like me"), most of my suggestions were received in a positive light. And very quickly, I was put in charge of interesting cases that enabled me to bring my ideas to fruition.

I felt a great weight had lifted from my shoulders.

Both my career and my feeling of happiness took off!

Quick fix

In the situation previously described, I had already been exposed to the international environment for a while, and no longer had an immediately negative reaction to my boss's blunt request for suggestions. A few months prior to that, I would have reacted defensively, as would most French people, I guess.

* * *

Confronted with such comments, I would have felt that I had lost face. Anyone in a similar position would have a negative reaction.

* * *

As Maya Angelou famously said, "I've learned that people will forget what you said, people will forget what you did, but people will never forget how you made them feel."

* * *

And losing face is one of the worst emotions you can feel.

In Summary

Throughout this book, it has become clear that we French are blessed with numerous gifts!

Our gifts:

- We are prepared to fight for justice in order to protect the vulnerable

- We have a thirst for culture and the greatest respect for knowledge

- We are good at complex reasoning and proud of our Cartesian logic

- Our critical flair prevents us from being led by the nose

In order to get the best out of us, you just have to overcome a few challenges

- **Challenge 1**: Help us move from Revolution to Evolution.

Encourage us to act rather than react. Bear with us. And don't forget that when the French protest, it's often because they are convinced of the justness of their cause.

- **Challenge 2**: Help us extract ourselves from the depths of culture in order to gain a broader view.

The French are philosophers at heart, literary buffs at the deepest level. Encourage us to gain perspective and to enjoy a more rounded panorama of the modern world.

- **Challenge 3**: Help us break our cycle of hypothesis—possible outcome—hypothesis—another possible outcome ...

Help us reach a conclusion and ideally a final decision by preventing us from 'reflecting' too much.

- **Challenge 4**: Help us step away from our built-in talent for criticism.

Lead us towards an inclusive approach enabling the knitting of relationships and weaving of ideas.

The Gallic Cooking-pot

Each of the four elements constituting the foundation of French education—the spirit of the French Revolution, the thirst for culture, the logic of Descartes, the talent for contradiction—comprises myriad advantages when used separately and in the right amount.

* * *

Combined together and served in large proportions, they create a cultural broth that can be difficult to digest. We all know that it only takes a pinch too much to make what was delightfully spicy go sour.

Remember the comic stories of Asterix and Obelix?

Our famous comic-book hero, Obelix, is as strong as an ox because he fell into the cauldron of magic potion when he was a tiny tot. When he is lifting logs or chasing wild boars he is using his power with purpose. At other times he uses his strength to excess.

* * *

The villagers have to keep reminding Obelix that he fell into the cauldron, and that his huge strength is excessive—both useful and dangerous. They do everything they can to prevent him from drinking any more potion.

* * *

Just like Obelix, we French run the risk of overdosing when we inhale the heady fumes of our cultural broth emanating from the Gallic cooking-pot.

* * *

So, be like the wise Gallic villagers and do your best to keep us away from too much intellectual nourishment.

What about you non-French?

1. Beware of generalisation
Can you lump the 60 million French people together? Obviously not.

* * *

Individuals within a group differ from each other, and it would be an over-simplification to automatically ascribe national or regional characteristics to them.

* * *

Nothing is more irritating than hearing somebody say, "How typically French" (or English, if that's your background), because it seeks to 'reduce' you to a predictable person functioning in exactly the same way as millions of other individuals.

* * *

Our personal characteristics, our family environment and our life experience make us all different from one another. Our actions are dictated by all those elements, plus the context in which they occur.

* * *

The personality traits described in this book only make up collective trends. They should be considered clichés, and as usual with clichés cannot be applied to specific individuals but only to groups observed as a whole from the outside.

* * *

Each encounter with a French person—or any person for that matter—will be unpredictable. You might recognise some of the personality traits described in this book, but certainly not all of them.

* * *

Be prepared for surprises and enjoy the exchange.

2. Separate intention from impact

Let us not forget that at the individual level, every action has an intention. The impact on others, however, is not necessarily linked to that intention. This is because both the sender and the receiver have their filters, made up of their own characteristics, family environment and life experience.

* * *

Herein lies the root of most conflicts and misunderstandings: something that you have said with a very positive intention can be interpreted by your counterpart in all sorts of ways.

For example, you say to a friend: "You look tired" with the intention of expressing your concern at their wellbeing. They might take this comment positively and thank you for your sympathy. Or they might take it badly and accuse you of making value-judgments on their appearance. In which case you can only reaffirm your good intentions, and make sure that next time you leave out commenting on how they look.

* * *

Other instances of the difference between intention and impact can be seen in the code of politeness according to various cultures.

* * *

If you give somebody a gift in France or in the UK, you would expect your host to open it in front of you and show some appreciation. In Egypt, on the other hand, it would be considered bad manners to open a gift in front of the donor.

* * *

In both cases, opening or not opening the gift is a sign of politeness by the recipient. As the giver, we need to be careful not to make assumptions about the recipient's reaction.

Anecdote

The smile of a weirdo?
After 30 years in Geneva, Sergei went back to Russia to visit his friends. Without thinking, he smiled at the people who joined him in the elevator in the first building he entered in Moscow.

The surprised, disapproving or even anxious looks he got in return reminded him that such a friendly attitude is not acceptable in his native country. The norm is to remain stony-faced towards strangers.

* * *

What we consider normal polite behaviour is interpreted as bizarre by the Russians.

Today Sergei laughs about the different attitude in the two countries. He realises that for the most part he has adapted to the customs of his country of residence.

3. Recognise your pre-conceived ideas

• We cling to our convictions

All over the planet, human beings hate being proved wrong. For some reason, we find it comforting to cling to our convictions.

* * *

In a conversation with someone, it is difficult to admit that we have made a mistake or that we might be wrong.

* * *

Even in situations where there is no external pressure, and when we know that change would be of benefit to us, we are so attached to our way of thinking that we have the greatest reluctance to letting go of our convictions.

- **We only see what we are looking for**

The clichés with which we label a group influence the way we perceive that same group. If we believe that Americans eat nothing but 'fatty food', we will do everything to confirm this belief. Imagine we are lunching with John, an American we have met for the first time.

When he orders a portion of fries with a salad and mineral water, all we focus on is those fries—a 'fatty food'—disregarding John's salad and mineral water.

* * *

As non-French, when you meet up with an individual French person, be careful not to label him or her with a number of supposedly typical national characteristics. If you do so, this will impede all the richness and uniqueness of a particular encounter with a complex individual. Give the relationship the space to flourish in its own way.

* * *

To establish a meaningful interaction between two people, each should be ready to accept the other person **and** feel they are accepted by the other person in the three dimensions of the human race:

- in some regards I am like all the others,
- in some regards I am like some of the others,
- in some regards I am like none of the others.

* * *

Keeping this in mind is a key to successful communication.

4. Recognise your influence on the perception you have of others

Flaws become self-generating when we ascribe them to others.

* * *

Suppose you tell someone they are clumsy. This remark will stress the person to such an extent that they will become ... clumsy. And the more they try to prove their dexterity, the more they will be stressed, and the clumsier they will become.

* * *

Imagine somebody saying, "The French are rude". Any French person hearing that will obviously answer the remark in a rude manner. The other person will be even more convinced that the French are rude. ... At the same time, the French person so accused will have no wish to divert them from that conviction.

* * *

If for you a pile of papers scattered on a desk is an indication of a chaotic mind, you will never be able to discover the potential organisational skills of the office worker concerned.

They might excel at project management and strategy planning, for example, and you will never see it.

The Magic Touch

In the introduction to this book you were promised that a touch of magic would be bestowed upon you, guaranteeing success in any encounter with French persons.

* * *

This magic is of course connected to our world-famous trump card: food. How could this not be the case? Our cuisine has been declared "World intangible heritage" by UNESCO.

* * *

Above all, we are the undisputed masters at producing bread. The *baguette* is the jewel of our craftsmanship, a national emblem, a source of well-deserved pride.

* * *

You will already be familiar with the nourishing properties of our *baguette*. Today, I am going to add a little touch of magic to it.

Let me be your fairy godmother; have complete faith in my supernatural powers.

As a French woman, bottle-fed with the broth ladled out of the Gallic cooking-pot, and having survived three decades working in international circles virtually unscathed, this is the proof that I am a super-being.

* * *

I am now solemnly endowing the *baguette* with a touch of magic. From now on, the mere thought of it will help you succeed in your interactions with us French.

* * *

Trust me, from this point forward you are fully equipped to enjoy enchanting relationships with us. Even if you happen to encounter a French person with the Obelix complex—one who keeps dunking their piece of *baguette* into the broth bubbling in the Gallic cooking-pot without limit—it will all go fabulously,

....I promise!

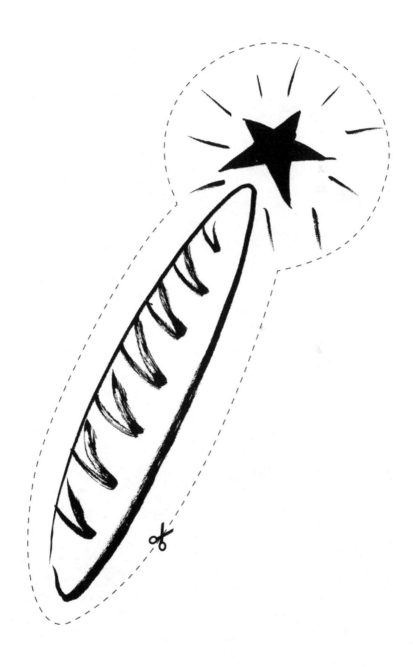

Enjoy France and … the French!
Good Luck!

Author and Illustrator Biographies

Marie-José Astre-Démoulin

Marie-José Astre-Démoulin is a French published author and a cross-cultural communication specialist. She has 20 years of experience within the United Nations at international level.

She now lives in Geneva and works as a consultant, delivering training sessions related with conflict management in universities and private companies all over the world.

She also acts as an Expert for cross-cultural communication issues in the Museum of Communication in Bern, Switzerland.

* * *

Jan Abellan

Jan Abellan is a designer, illustrator, photographer and professional video maker. He graduated from Ecole cantonale d'art de Lausanne (ECAL) in 2011. He won the Swiss Design Award in 2012. He is the co-founder of a design studio based in Paris and Lausanne. His clients include Swiss and international brands involved in the luxury and cultural markets. He is also an editorial designer and owner of a letterpress printing company in Lausanne, Switzerland.

photo credits: Simon de Sarzens

Note to the reader

Thank you for purchasing *The Gallic Cooking-Pot*. Our sincere hope is that you derived as much pleasure from reading this book as we have in creating it.

If you have a few moments, please feel free to add your review of the book to your favourite online site for feedback.

Also, if you would like to connect with our upcoming works, please visit our websites.

Sincerely,

Marie-José Astre-Démoulin and Jan Abellan

http://mjdastree.123website.ch/

http://wwwjanabellan.com

BUSINESS
BOOKS

Business Books

Business Books publishes practical guides
and insightful non-fiction for beginners and professionals.
Covering aspects from management skills, leadership and
organizational change to positive work environments, career
coaching and self-care for managers, our books are a valuable
addition to those working in the world of business.

15 Ways to Own Your Future
Take Control of Your Destiny in Business and in Life
Michael Khouri
A 15-point blueprint for creating better collaboration, enjoyment,
and success in business and in life.

Paperback: 978-1-78535-300-0 ebook: 978-1-78535-301-7

The Common Excuses of the Comfortable Compromiser
Understanding Why People Oppose Your Great Idea
Matt Crossman
Comfortable compromisers block the way of anyone trying to
change anything. This is your guide to their common excuses.

Paperback: 978-1-78099-595-3 ebook: 978-1-78099-596-0

The Failing Logic of Money
Duane Mullin
Money is wasteful and cruel, causes war, crime and dysfunctional
feudalism. Humankind needs happiness, peace and abundance. So
banish money and use technology and knowledge to rid the world
of war, crime and poverty.

Paperback: 978-1-84694-259-4 ebook: 978-1-84694-888-6

Mastering the Mommy Track
Juggling Career and Kids in Uncertain Times
Erin Flynn Jay
Mastering the Mommy Track tells the stories of everyday working
mothers, the challenges they have faced, and lessons learned.

Paperback: 978-1-78099-123-8 ebook: 978-1-78099-124-5

Modern Day Selling
Unlocking Your Hidden Potential
Brian Barfield
Learn how to reconnect sales associates with customers and unlock hidden sales potential.
Paperback: 978-1-78099-457-4 ebook: 978-1-78099-458-1

The Most Creative, Escape the Ordinary, Excel at Public Speaking Book Ever
All The Help You Will Ever Need in Giving a Speech
Philip Theibert
The 'everything you need to give an outstanding speech' book, complete with original material written by a professional speech-writer.
Paperback: 978-1-78099-672-1 ebook: 978-1-78099-673-8

Readers of ebooks can buy or view any of these bestsellers by clicking on the live link in the title. Most titles are published in paperback and as an ebook. Paperbacks are available in traditional bookshops. Both print and ebook formats are available online.
Find more titles and sign up to our readers' newsletter at
http://www.jhpbusiness-books.com/
Facebook: https://www.facebook.com/JHPNonFiction/
Twitter: @JHPNonFiction